Disney SONGS
FOR MALE SINGERS
10 ALL-TIME FAVORITES

To access online audio, visit:
www.halleonard.com/mylibrary

Enter Code
1512-3606-6134-5570

Hal•Leonard®
7777 W. Bluemound Rd. P.O. Box 13819 Milwaukee, WI 53213

D0584736

ISBN 978-1-5400-0427-7

In Australia Contact:
Hal Leonard Australia Pty. Ltd.
4 Lentara Court
Cheltenham, Victoria, 3192 Australia
Email: ausadmin@halleonard.com.au

Visit Hal Leonard Online at
www.halleonard.com

THE BARE NECESSITIES
from THE JUNGLE BOOK

Words and Music by
TERRY GILKYSON

Look for the bare ne - ces - si - ties, __ the sim - ple, bare ne -

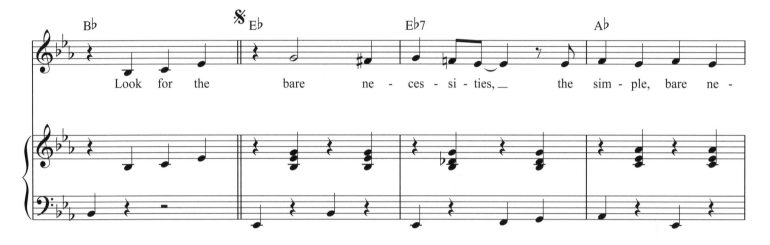

ces - si - ties. __ For - get a - bout __ your wor - ries and your strife.

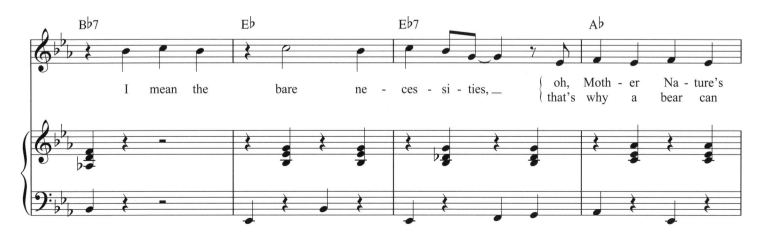

I mean the bare ne - ces - si - ties, __ { oh, Moth - er Na - ture's / that's why a bear can

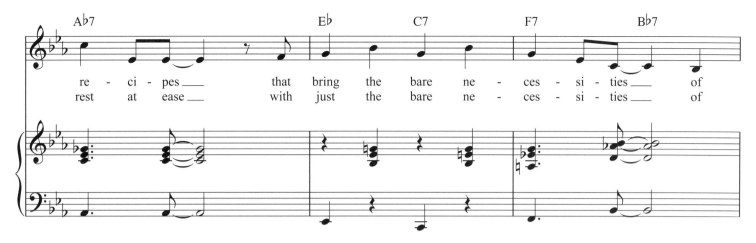

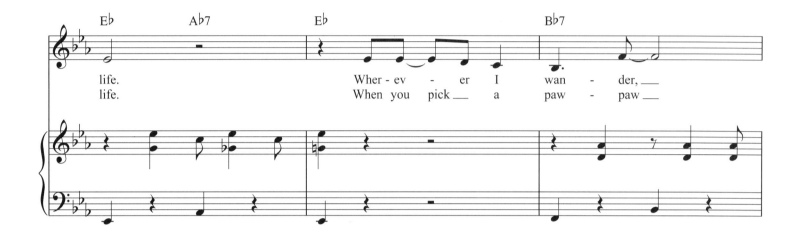

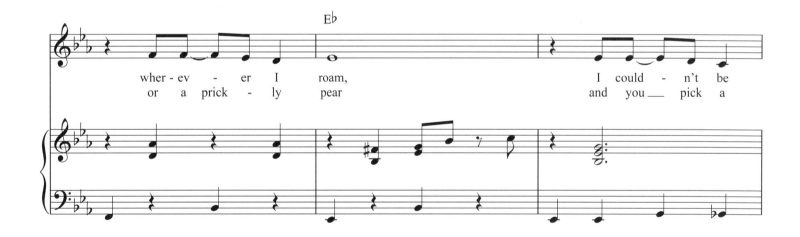

To Coda ⊕

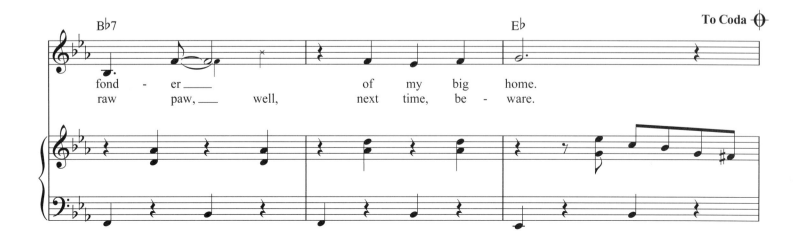

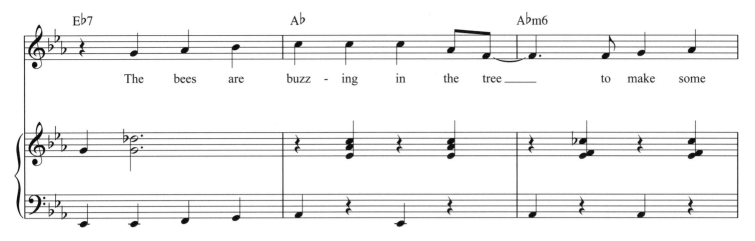

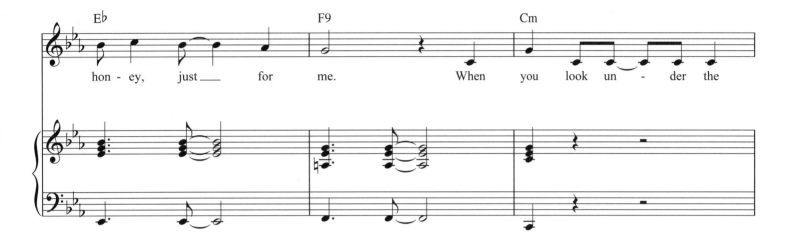

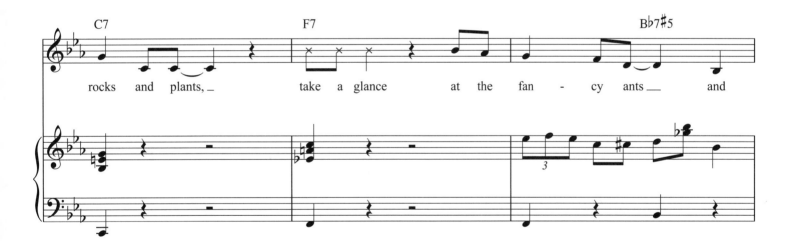

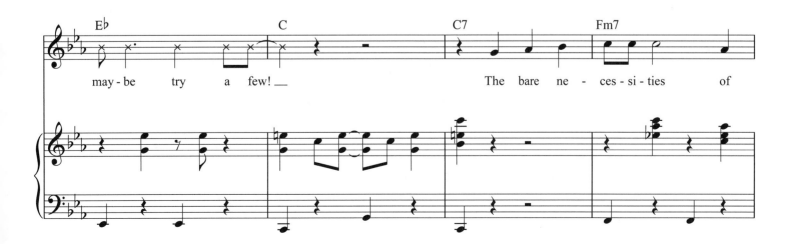

life will come to you. ___ They'll come to you. ___

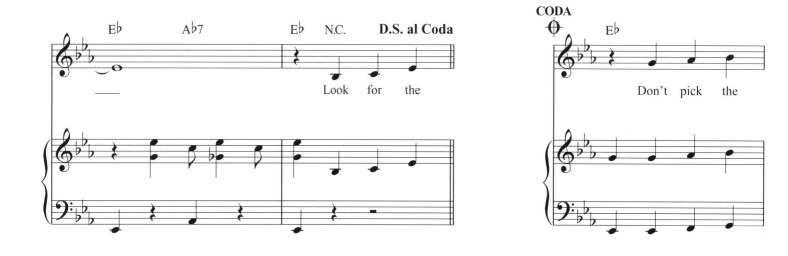

___ Look for the

CODA

Don't pick the

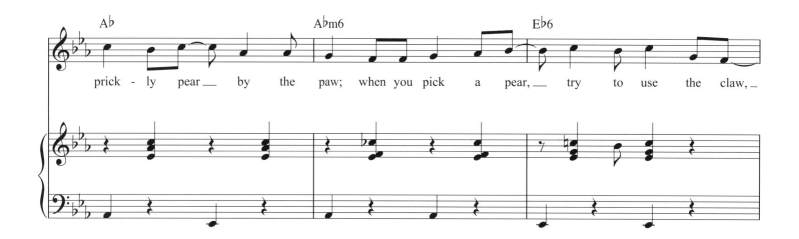

prick - ly pear ___ by the paw; when you pick a pear, ___ try to use the claw, ___

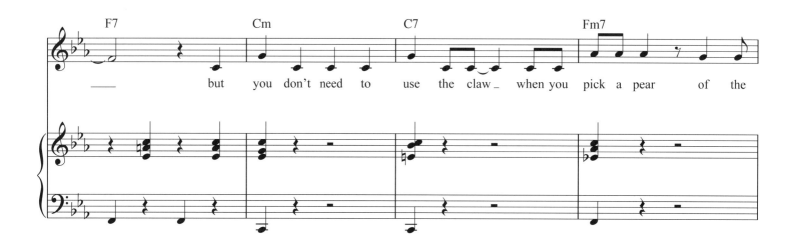

___ but you don't need to use the claw ___ when you pick a pear of the

FRIEND LIKE ME
from ALADDIN

Music by ALAN MENKEN
Lyrics by HOWARD ASHMAN

Bright Two-beat

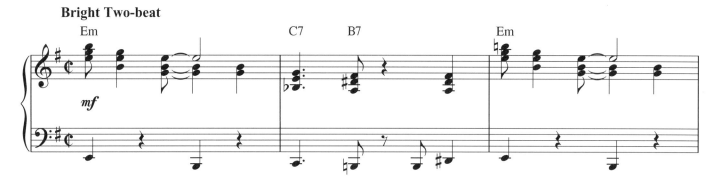

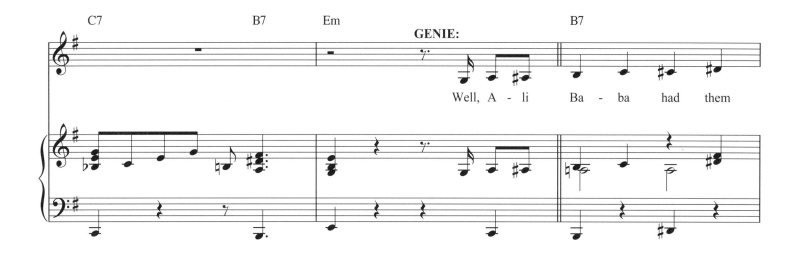

Well, A - li Ba - ba had them

for - ty thieves. She - he - ra - za - de had a thou - sand tales.

But, mas-ter, you in luck 'cause up your sleeves_ you got a

brand of mag-ic nev-er fails.____ You got some pow-er in your

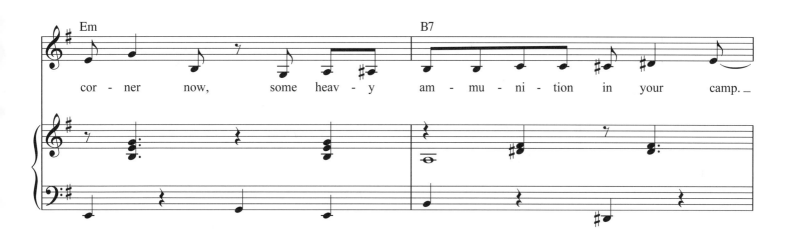

cor-ner now, some heav-y am-mu-ni-tion in your camp._

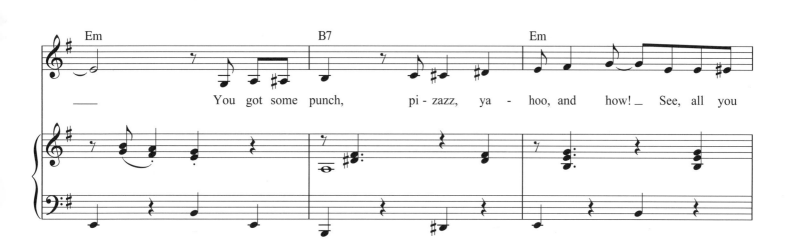

____ You got some punch, pi-zazz, ya-hoo, and how!_ See, all you

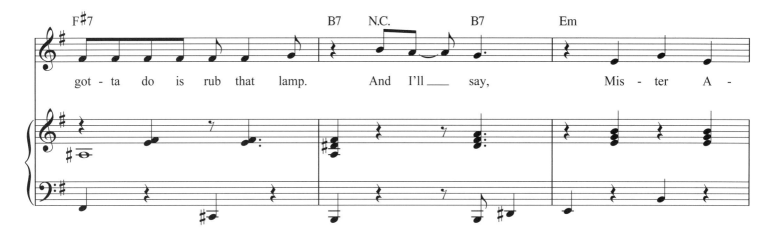

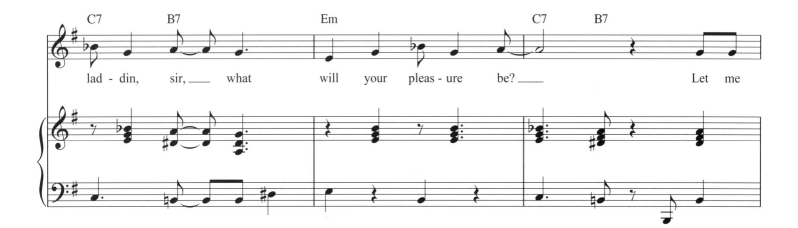

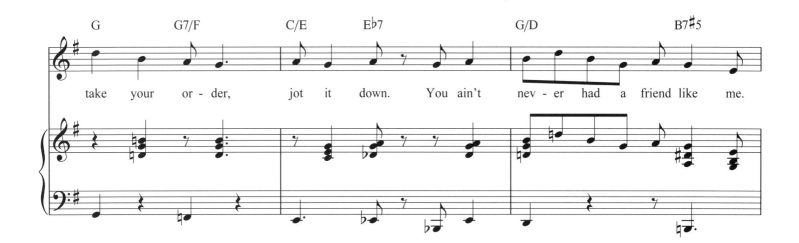

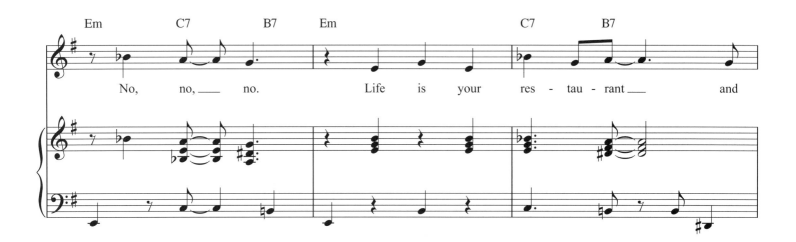

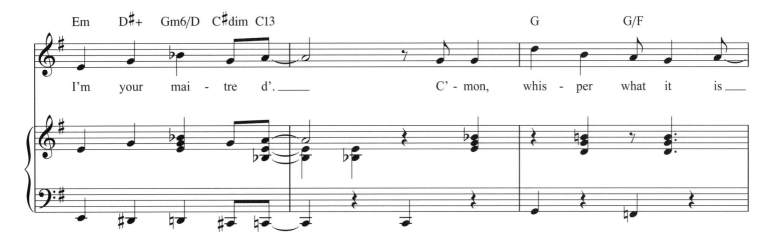

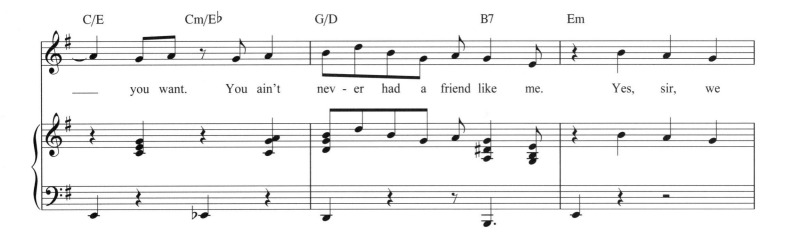

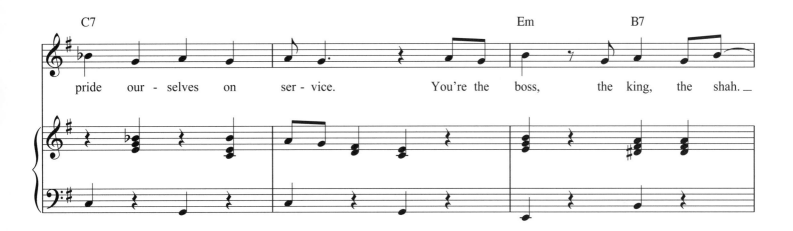

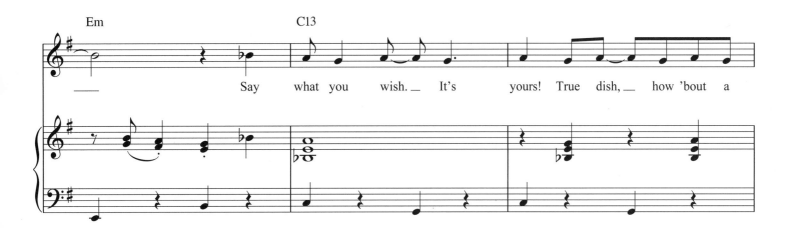

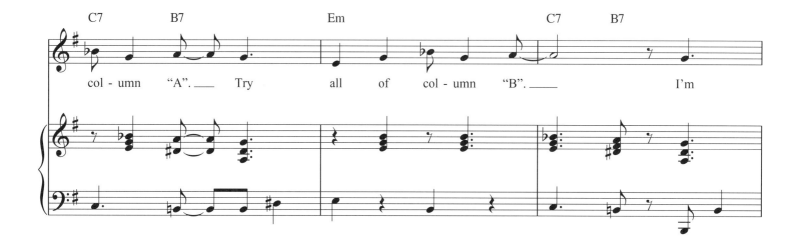

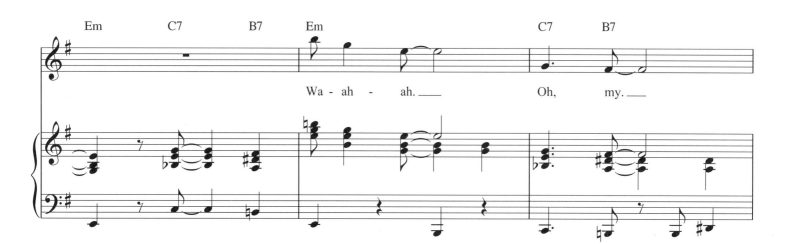

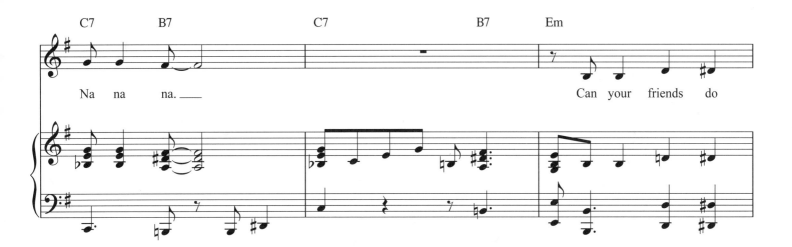

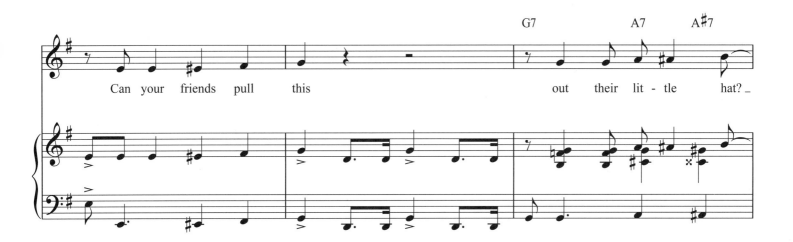

Can your friends _ go poof?

Well, look-y here. ____ Can your friends go

ab-ra-ca-dab-ra, let 'er rip, and then make the suck-er dis-ap - pear?

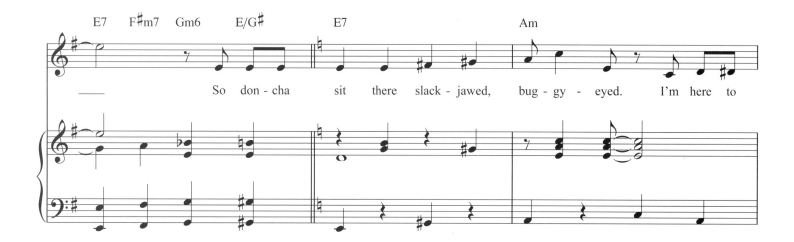

____ So don-cha sit there slack-jawed, bug-gy-eyed. I'm here to

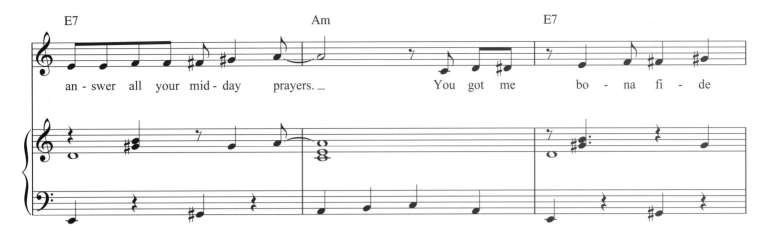

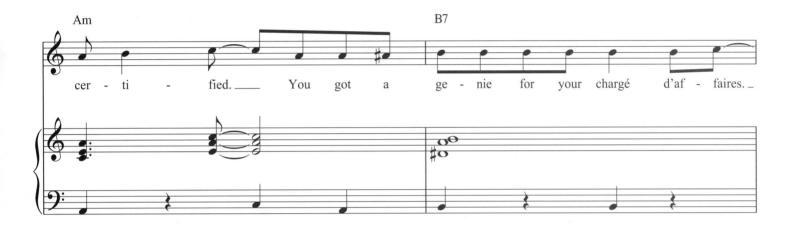

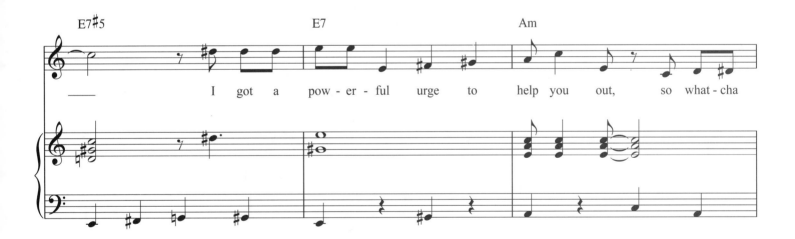

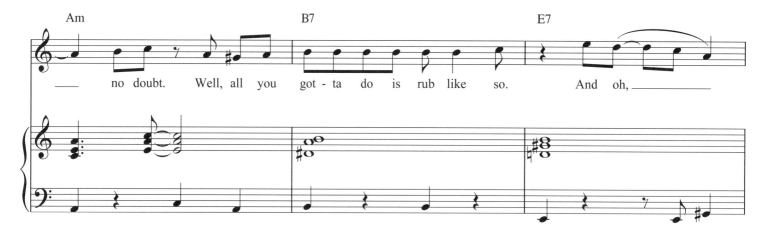

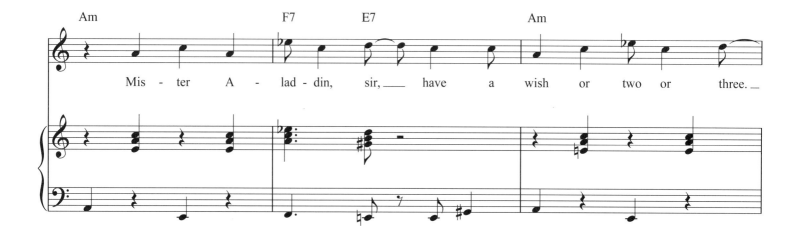

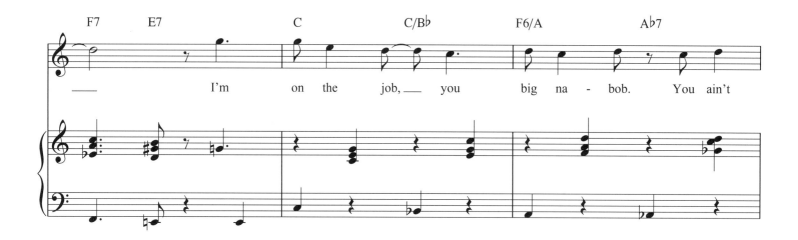

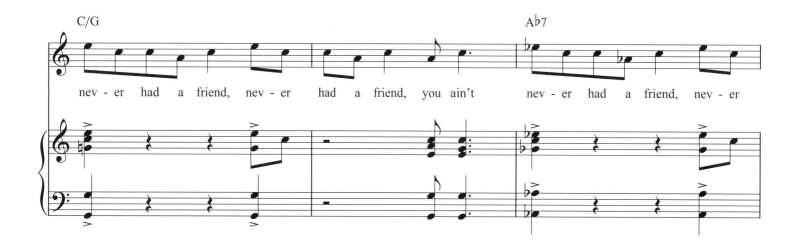

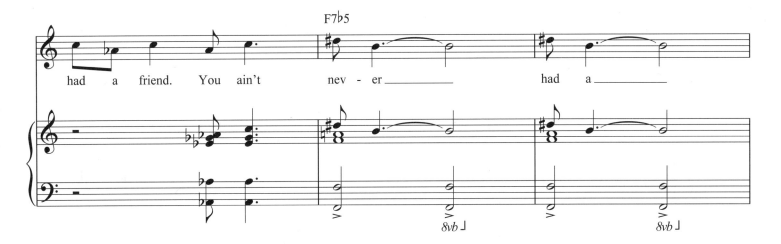

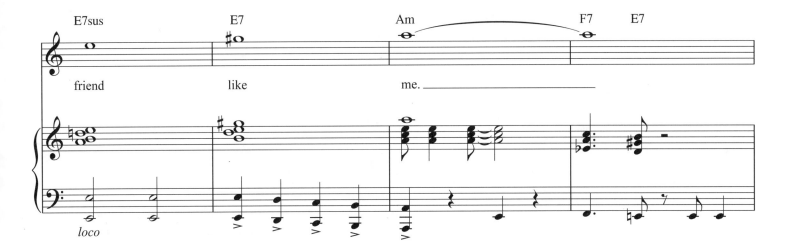

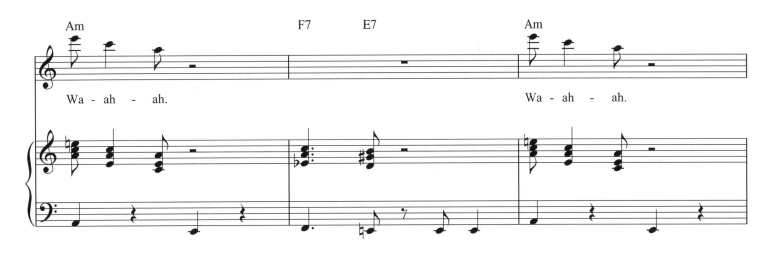

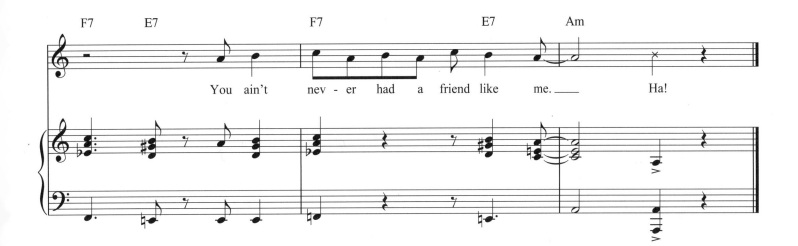

GASTON
from BEAUTY AND THE BEAST

Music by ALAN MENKEN
Lyrics by HOWARD ASHMAN

Rowdy barroom Waltz

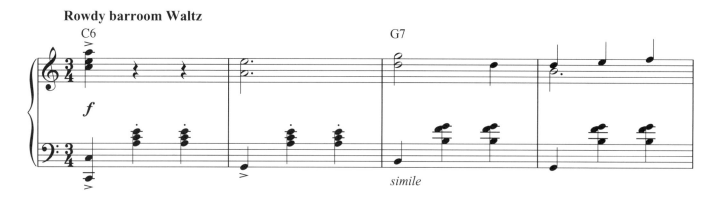

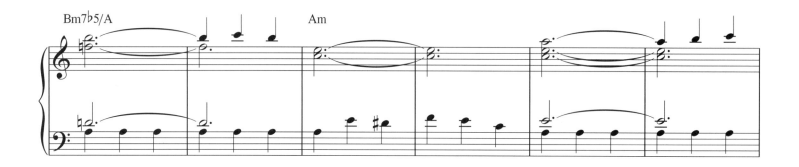

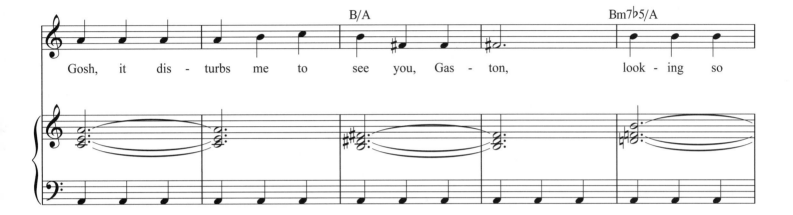

Gosh, it dis - turbs me to see you, Gas - ton, look - ing so

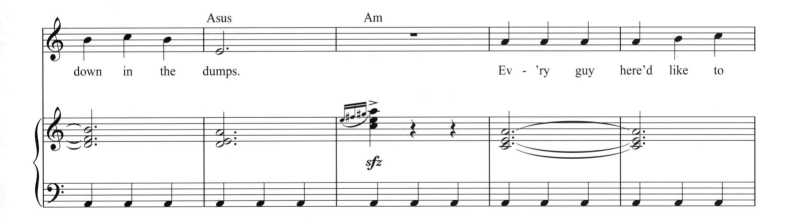

down in the dumps. Ev - 'ry guy here'd like to

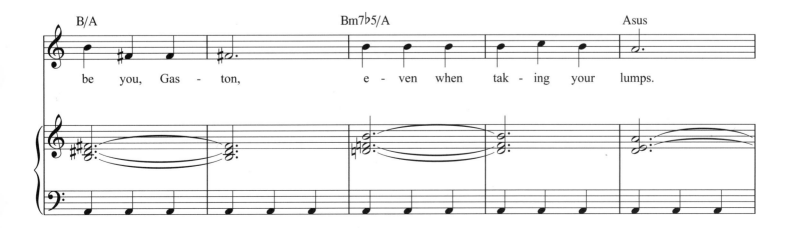

be you, Gas - ton, e - ven when tak - ing your lumps.

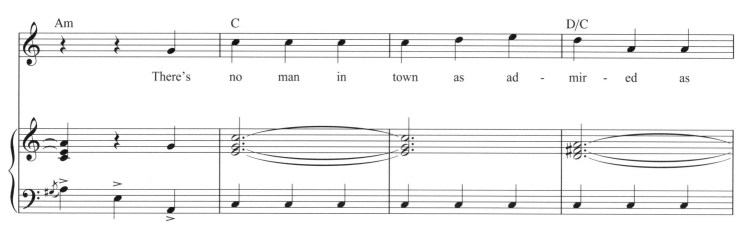

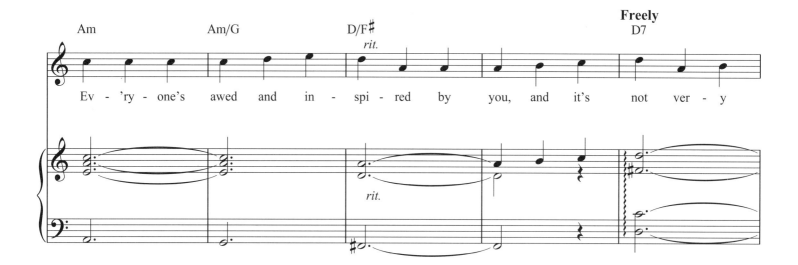

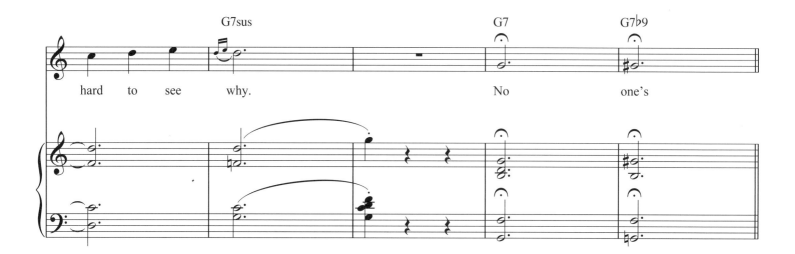

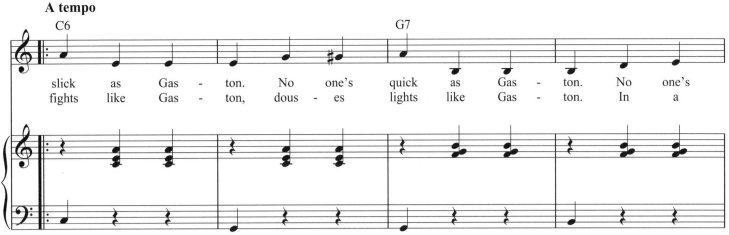

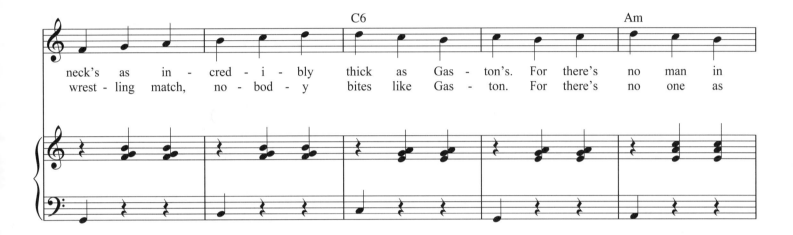

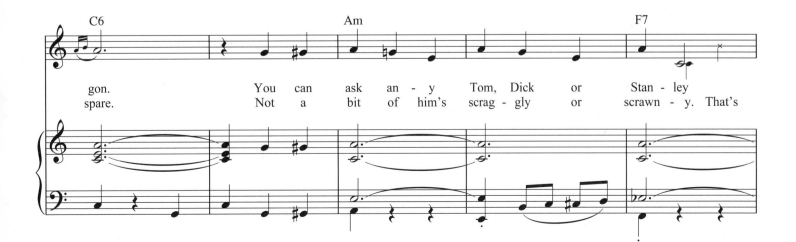

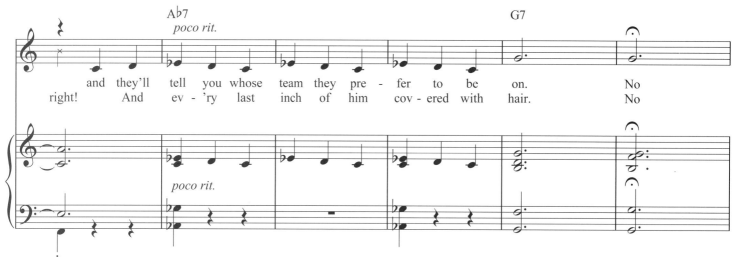

and they'll tell you whose team they pre - fer to be on. No
right! And ev - 'ry last inch of him cov - ered with hair. No

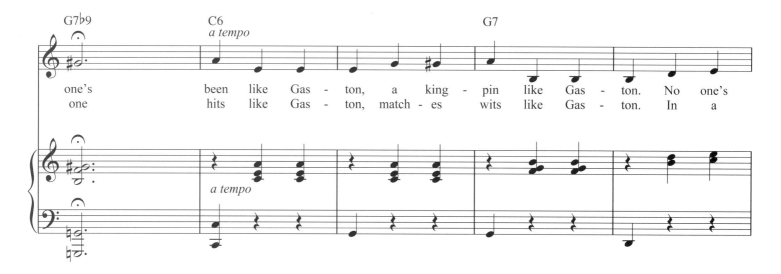

one's been like Gas - ton, a king - pin like Gas - ton. No one's
one hits like Gas - ton, match - es wits like Gas - ton. In a

got a swell cleft in his chin like Gas - ton. As a spec - i - men,
spit - ting match, no - bod - y spits like Gas - ton. He's es - pe - cial - ly

yes, he's in - tim - i - dat - ing! My, what a guy, that Gas -
good as ex - pec - tor - a - ting. Ptoo - ey! Ten points for Gas -

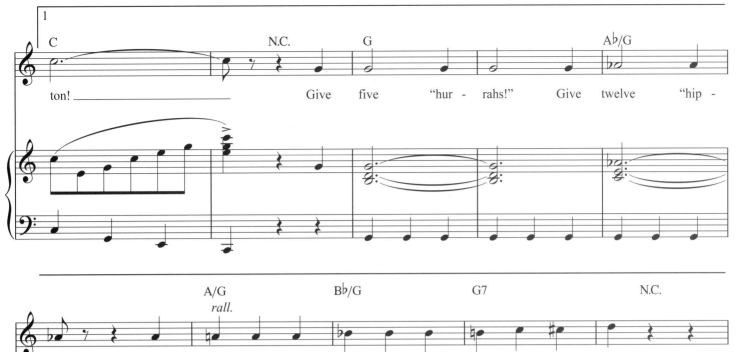

ton! _____ Give five "hur - rahs!" Give twelve "hip -

hips! ____ Gas - ton is the best and the rest is all drips!

No one ton! _____ When he was a lad he ate

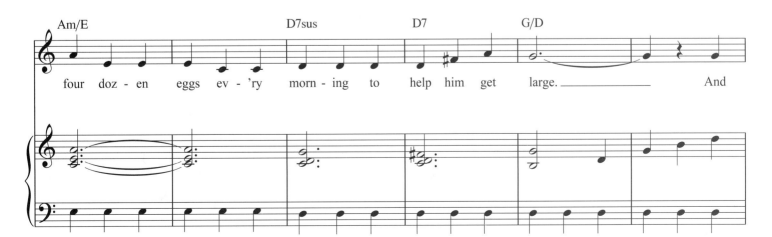

four doz - en eggs ev - 'ry morn - ing to help him get large. _____ And

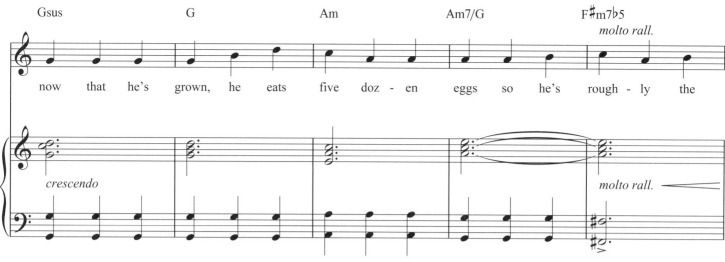

now that he's grown, he eats five doz-en eggs so he's rough-ly the

size of a barge! No one

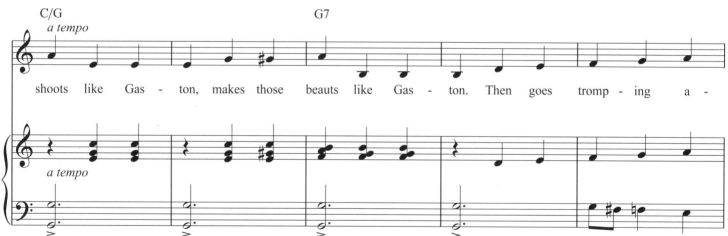

shoots like Gas - ton, makes those beauts like Gas - ton. Then goes tromp-ing a -

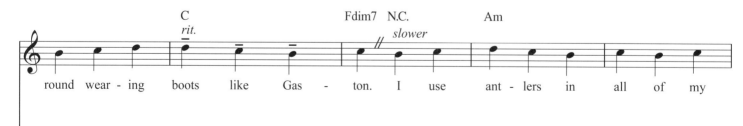

round wear-ing boots like Gas - ton. I use ant-lers in all of my

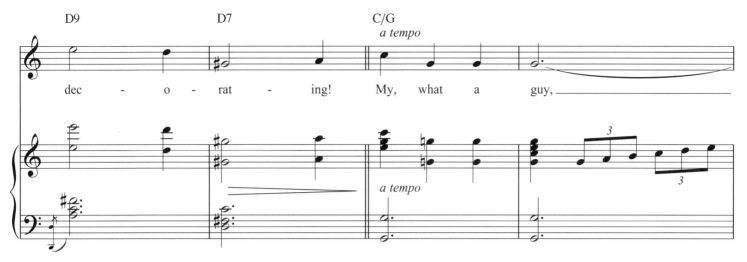

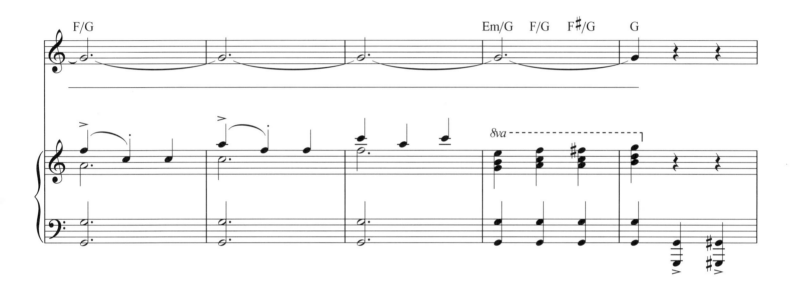

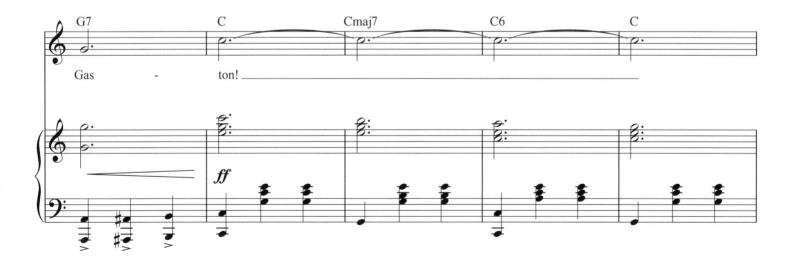

GO THE DISTANCE
from HERCULES

Music by ALAN MENKEN
Lyrics by DAVID ZIPPEL

Moderate Ballad

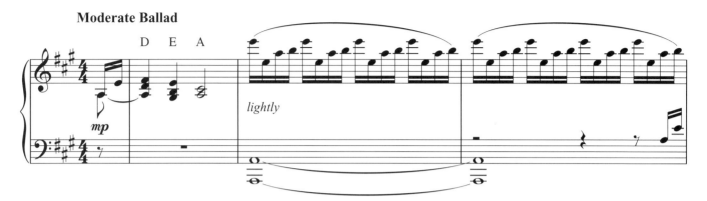

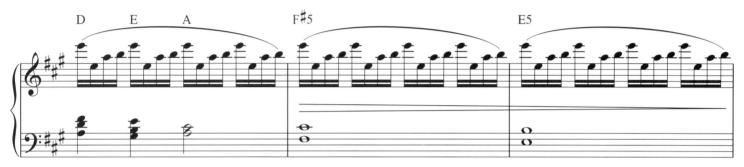

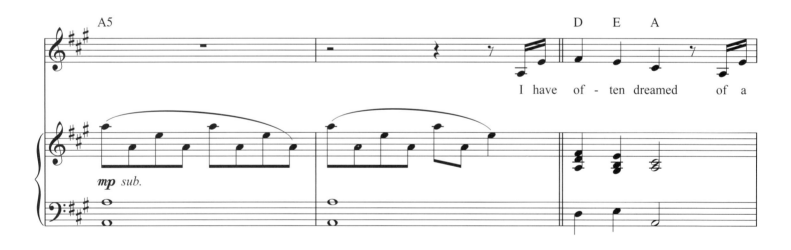

I have of-ten dreamed of a

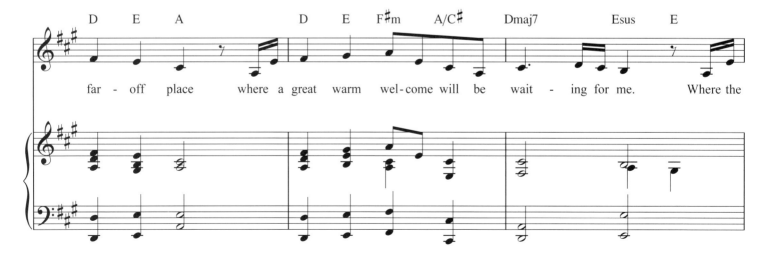

far - off place where a great warm wel-come will be wait - ing for me. Where the

crowds will cheer when they see my face, and a voice keeps say-ing this is

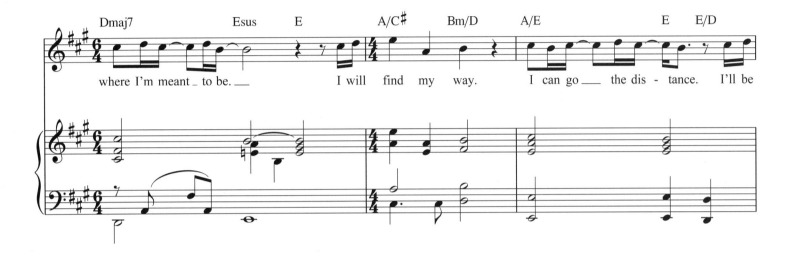

where I'm meant _ to be. _ I will find my way. I can go ___ the dis - tance. I'll be

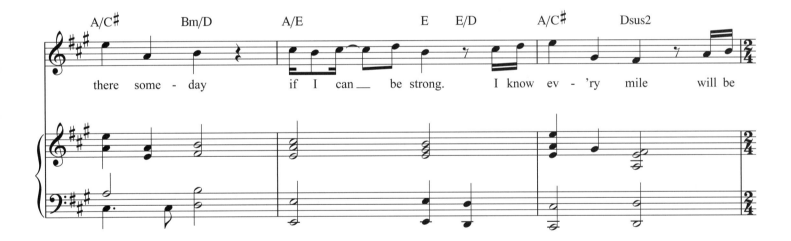

there some - day if I can _ be strong. I know ev - 'ry mile will be

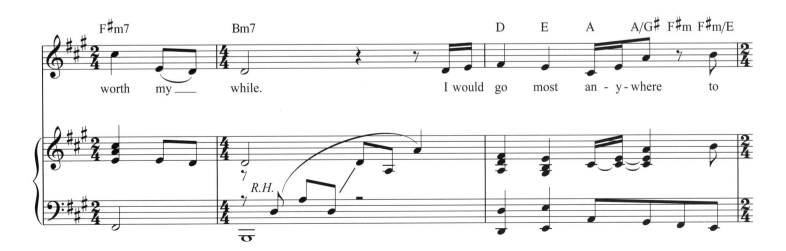

worth my ___ while. I would go most an - y-where to

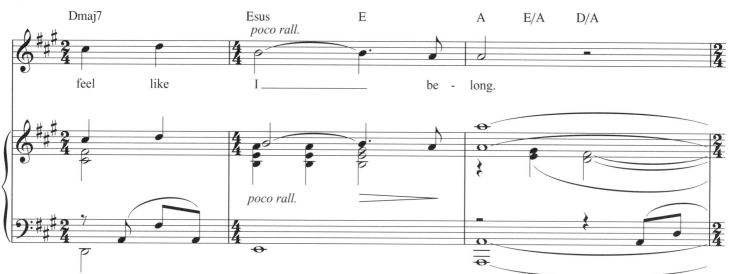

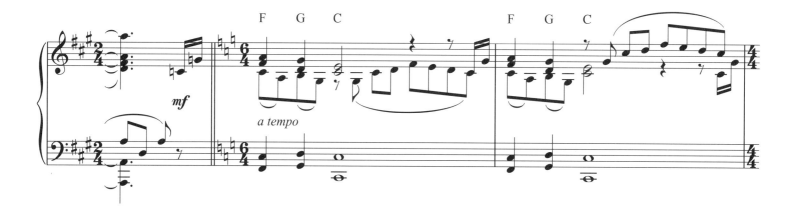

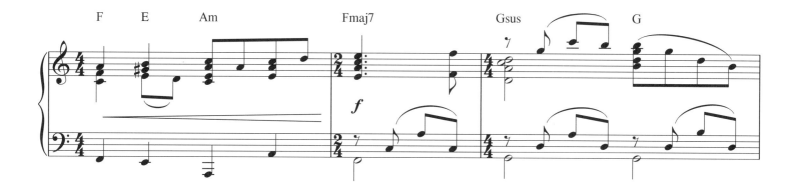

care how far, some-how I'll __ be strong. I know ev-'ry mile will be

worth my while. I would go most an-y-where to

find where I be - long.

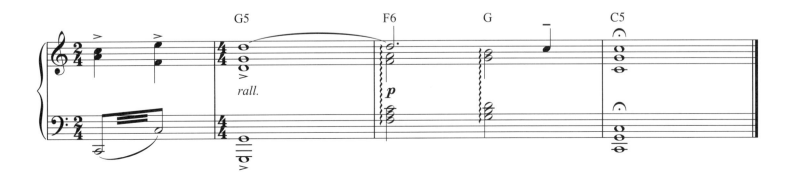

LES POISSONS
from THE LITTLE MERMAID

Music by ALAN MENKEN
Lyrics by HOWARD ASHMAN

Bright Waltz

Les Pois - sons, les pois -

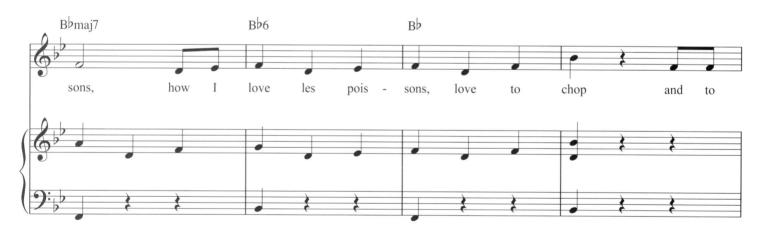

sons, how I love les pois - sons, love to chop and to

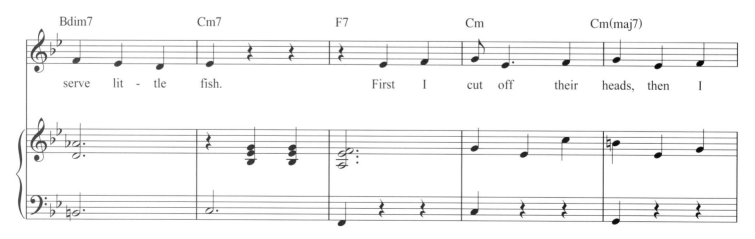

serve lit - tle fish. First I cut off their heads, then I

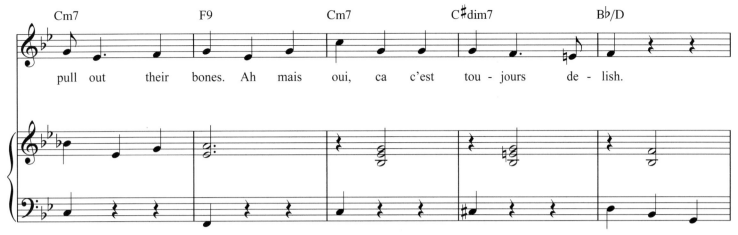

pull out their bones. Ah mais oui, ca c'est tou - jours de - lish.

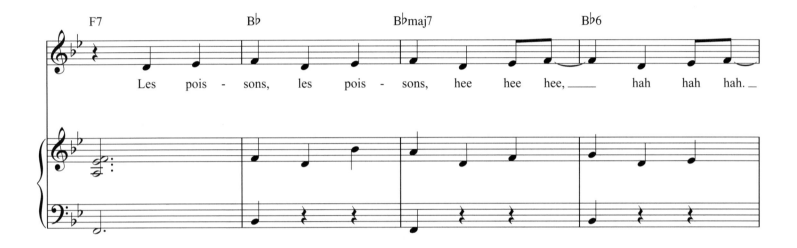

Les pois - sons, les pois - sons, hee hee hee, _____ hah hah hah. _

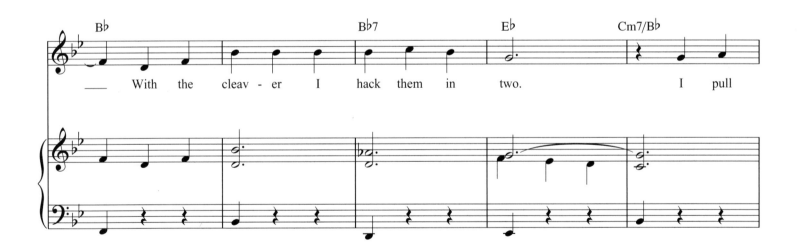

_ With the cleav - er I hack them in two. I pull

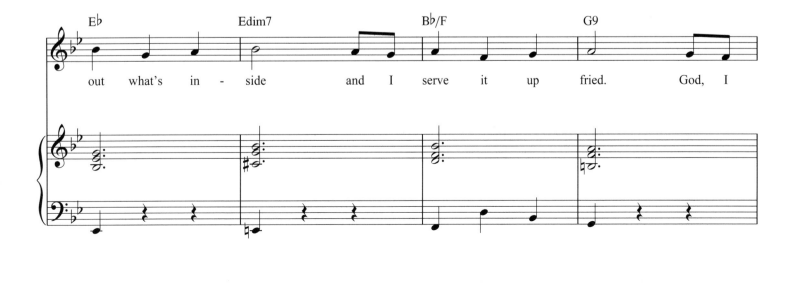

out what's in - side and I serve it up fried. God, I

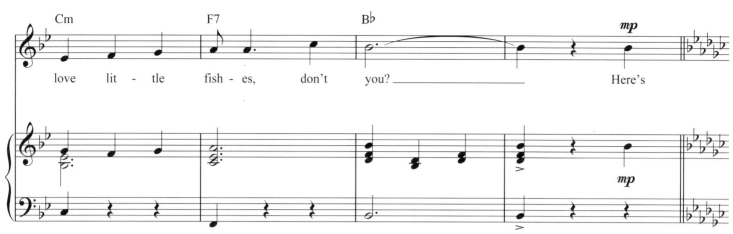

love lit - tle fish - es, don't you? _____ Here's

some - thing for tempt - ing the pal - ate, _____ pre - pared in the

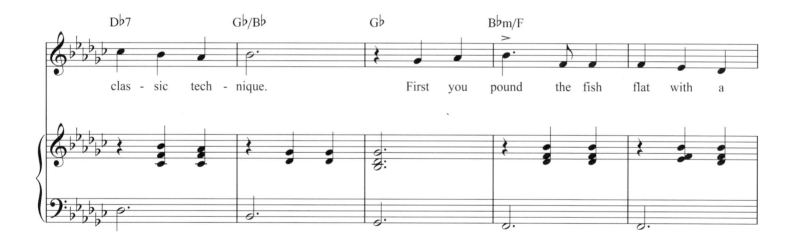

clas - sic tech - nique. First you pound the fish flat with a

mal - let. _____ Then you slash through the skin, give the bel - ly a

slice, then you rub some salt in 'cause that makes it taste

nice. Sa - cre bleu! What is this? How on earth could I

"Tout alors. I have missed one!"

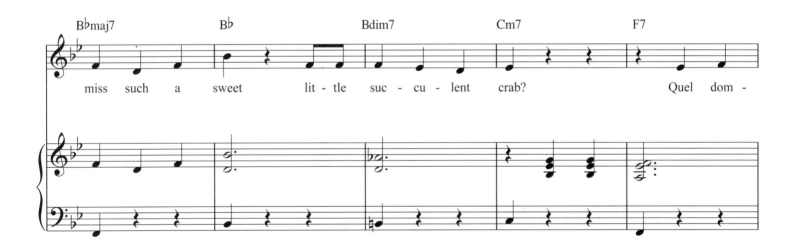

miss such a sweet lit - tle suc - cu - lent crab? Quel dom -

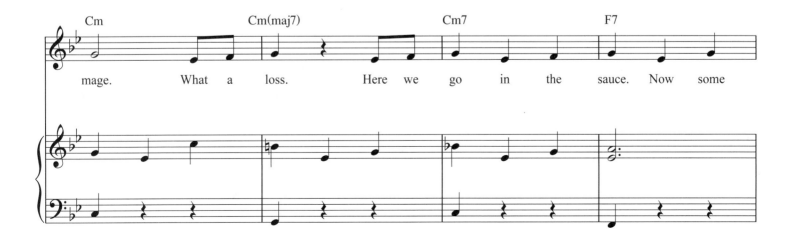

mage. What a loss. Here we go in the sauce. Now some

36

flour ___ I think, just a dab. Now I stuff you with

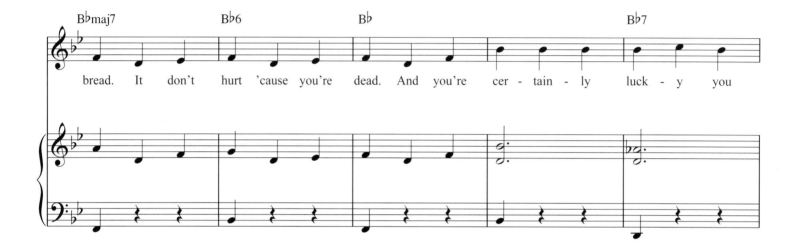

bread. It don't hurt 'cause you're dead. And you're cer - tain - ly luck - y you

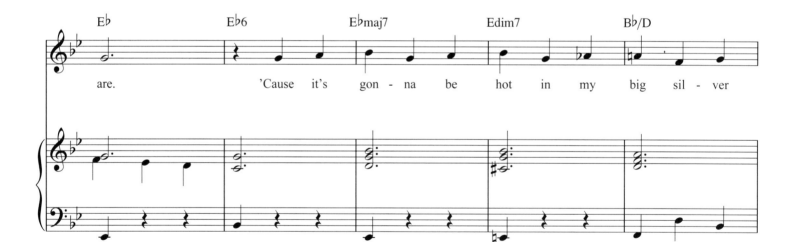

are. 'Cause it's gon - na be hot in my big sil - ver

pot. Too - dle - loo, mon pois - son, au re - voir!

PROUD OF YOUR BOY

from ALADDIN

Music by ALAN MENKEN
Lyrics by HOWARD ASHMAN

With determination, poco rubato

good, cross his stu-pid heart... Make good and fi-nal-ly make you____ proud of your

Moving forward

boy!

Poco più mosso

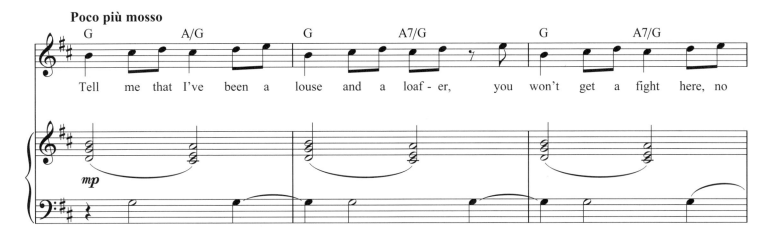

Tell me that I've been a louse and a loaf-er, you won't get a fight here, no

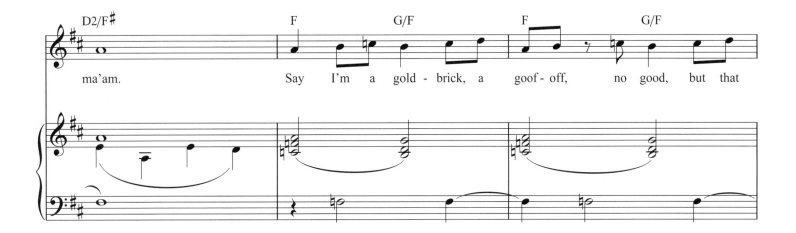

ma'am. Say I'm a gold-brick, a goof-off, no good, but that

40

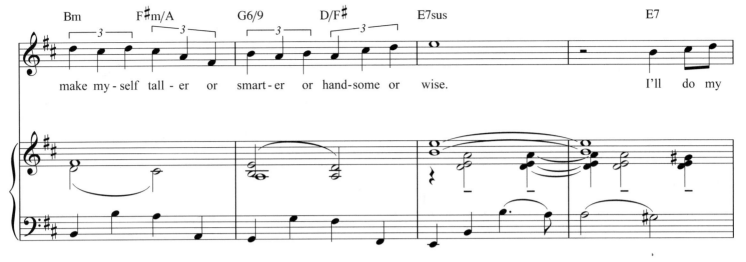

make my-self tall-er or smart-er or hand-some or wise. I'll do my

best, what else can I do? Since I was-n't born per - fect like Dad or you,

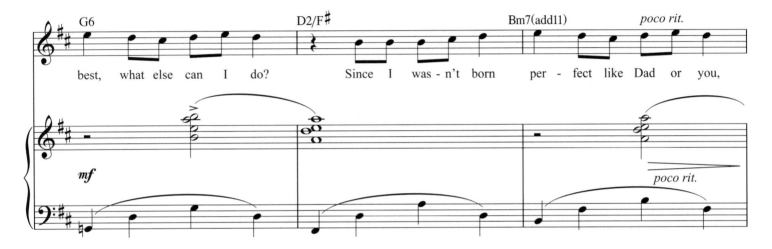

Mom, I will try to, try hard to make you proud of your

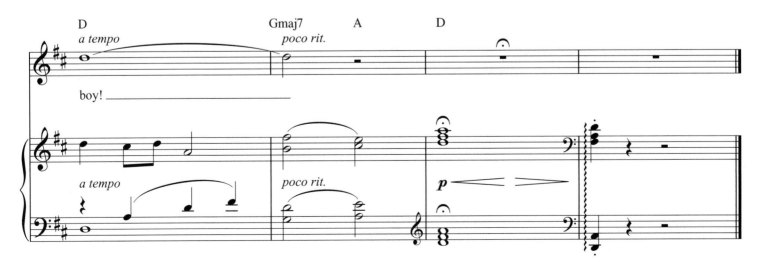

boy! _____

SANTA FE
from NEWSIES

Music by ALAN MENKEN
Lyrics by JACK FELDMAN

Freely

So that's what they call ___ a fam - 'ly ___ moth-er, daugh-ter, ___ fa - ther, son. ___ Guess that ev - 'ry-thing ___ you heard a - bout ___ is true. So you ain't got an - y fam - 'ly. ___ Well, who

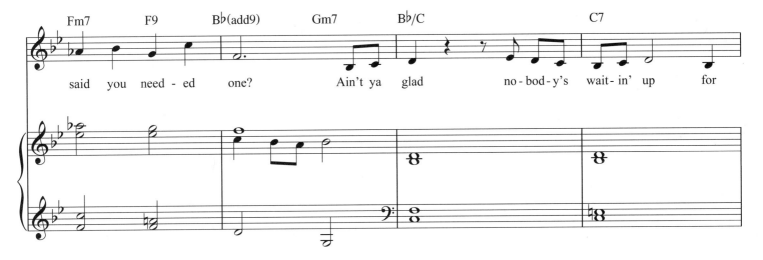

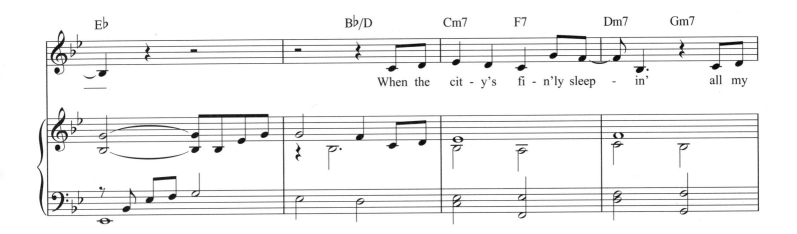

thoughts be - gin to stray ___ and I'm on the train that's bound for San - ta Fe. ___

And I'm free like the wind, like I'm

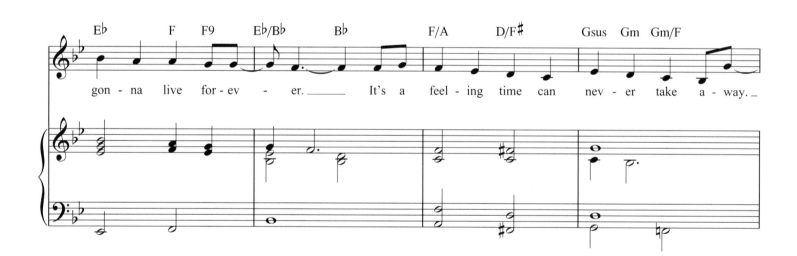

gon - na live for - ev - er. ___ It's a feel - ing time can nev - er take a - way.

All I need's a few more dol - lars ___ and I'm

out-ta here to stay.___ Dreams come true. Yes, they do_____ in San-ta

Somewhat faster

Fe._____

Where does it say you got-ta live and

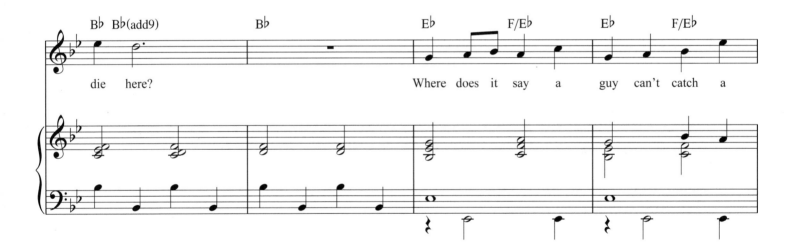

die here?

Where does it say a guy can't catch a

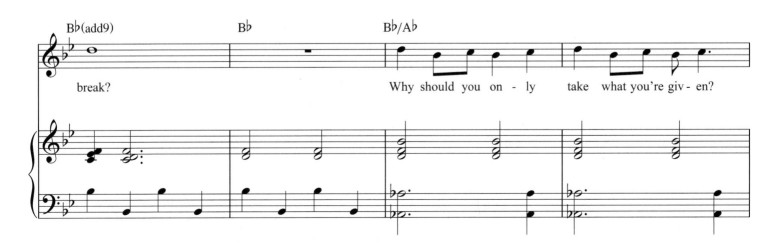

break?

Why should you on-ly take what you're giv-en?

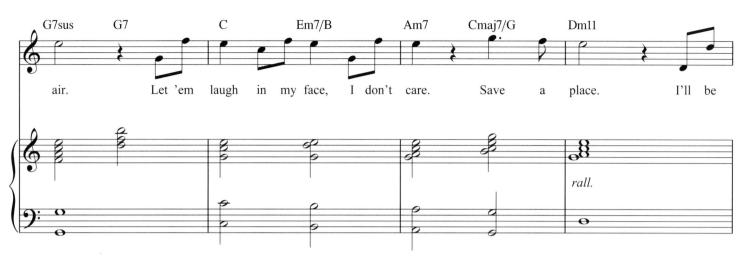

air.　Let 'em　laugh　in　my　face,　I　don't　care.　Save　a　place.　I'll be

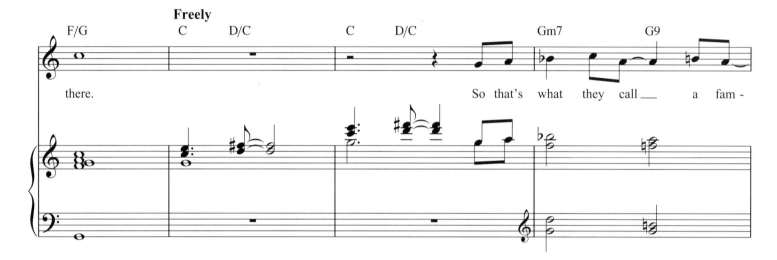

Freely

there.　So　that's　what　they　call ___ a　fam-

-'ly.　Ain't　you　glad　you　ain't _ that　way?　Ain't　you　glad　you　got　a

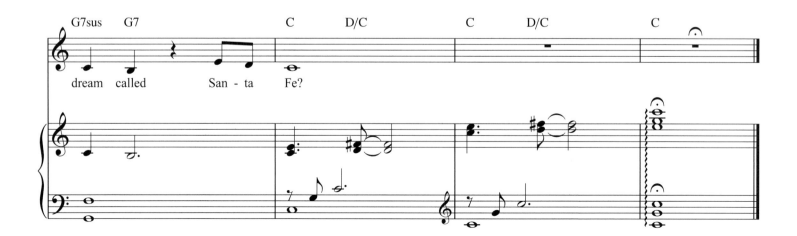

dream　called　San-　ta　Fe?

STRANGERS LIKE ME*

from TARZAN™

Words and Music by
PHIL COLLINS

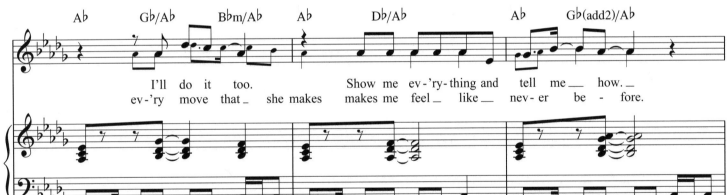

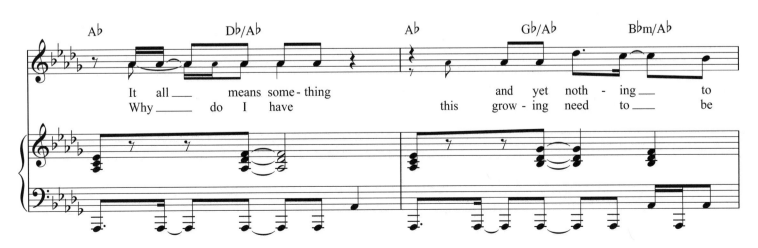

50

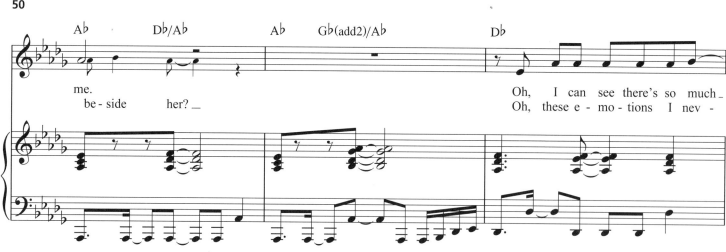

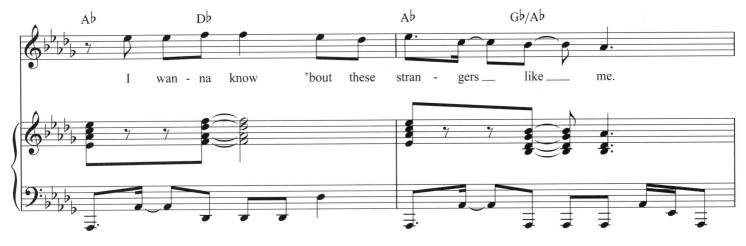

I wan - na know 'bout these stran - gers ___ like ___ me.

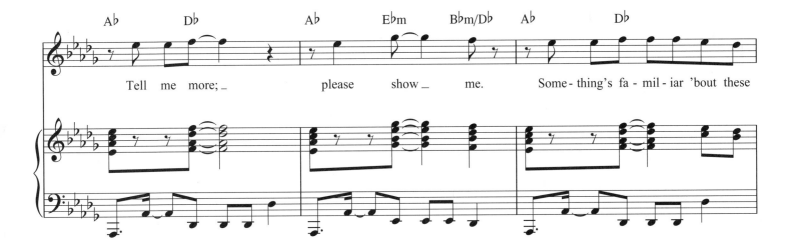

Tell me more; ___ please show ___ me. Some - thing's fa - mil - iar 'bout these

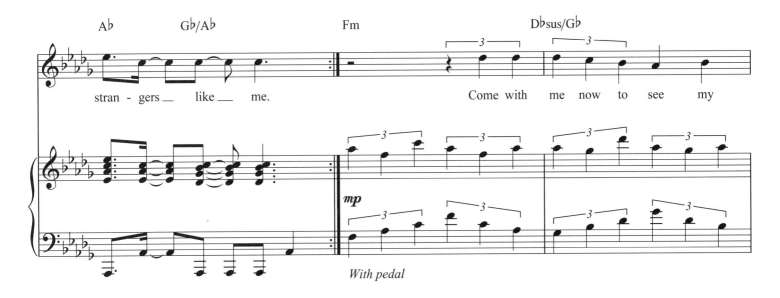

stran - gers ___ like ___ me. Come with me now to see my

With pedal

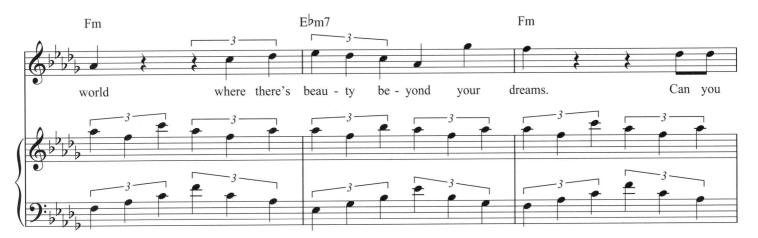

world where there's beau - ty be - yond your dreams. Can you

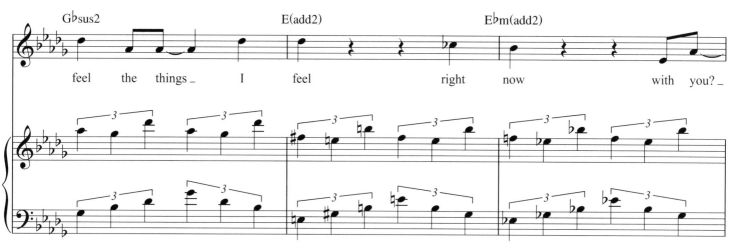

feel the things _ I feel right now with you? _

_ Take my hand; There's a

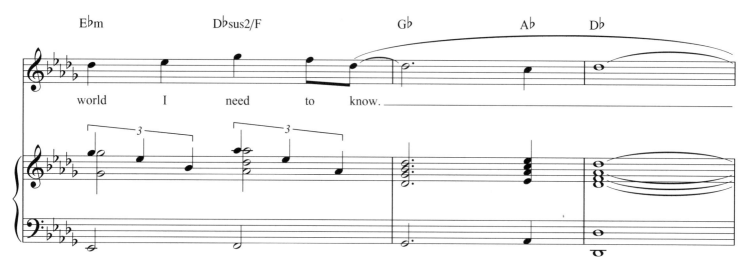

world I need to know. _

_ I wan-na know. Can you show _ me?

I wan-na know 'bout these stran-gers _ like _ me. Tell me more; _

please show _ me. Some-thing's fa - mil - iar 'bout these

stran - gers _ like _ me. I wan - na

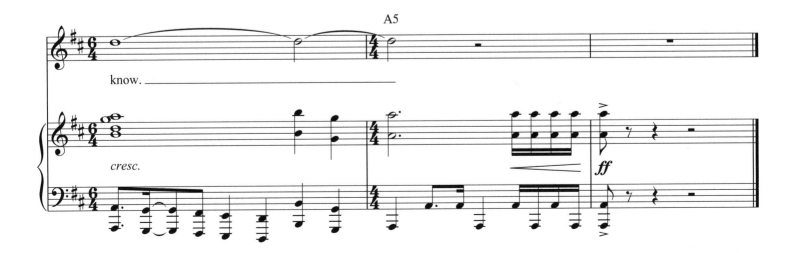

know. _

cresc.

ff

YOU'VE GOT A FRIEND IN ME

from TOY STORY

Music and Lyrics by
RANDY NEWMAN

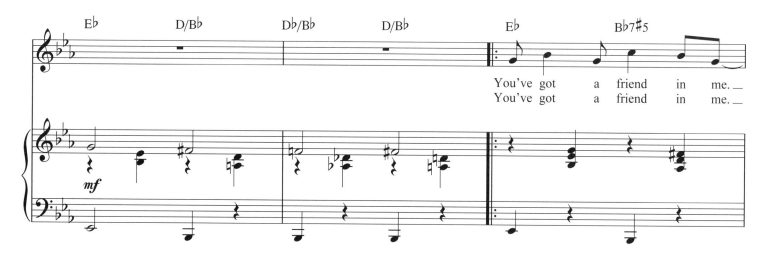

You've got a friend in me.___
You've got a friend in me.___

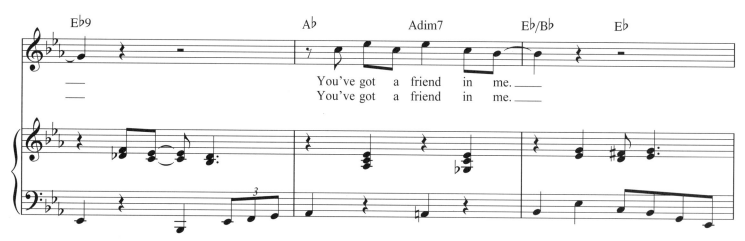

You've got a friend in me.___
You've got a friend in me.___

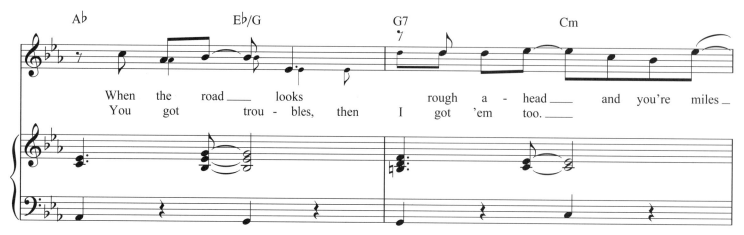

When the road___ looks rough a-head___ and you're miles___
You got trou-bles, then I got 'em too.___

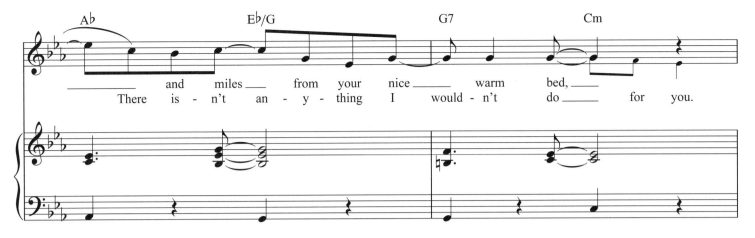

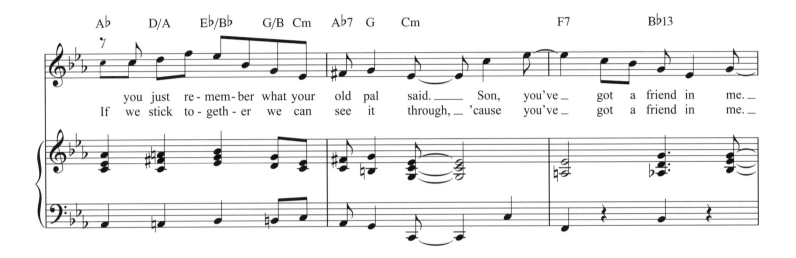

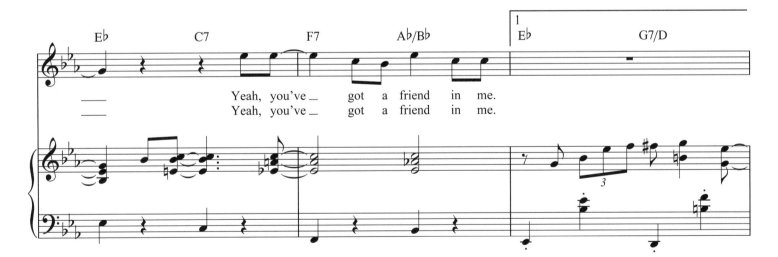

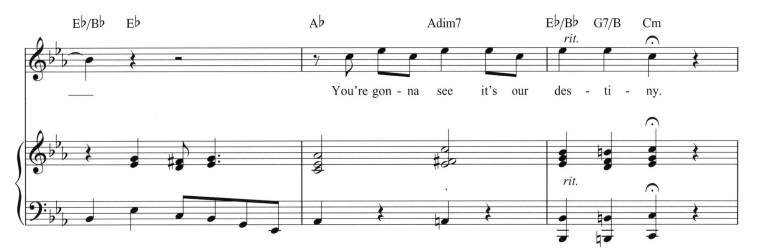

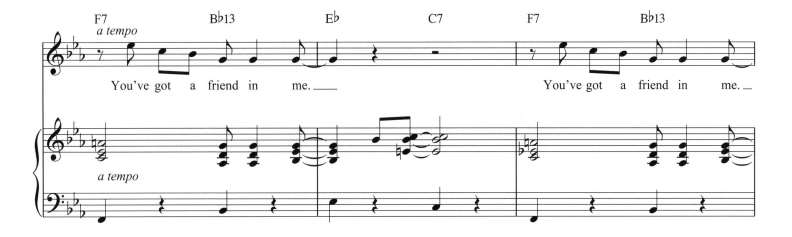

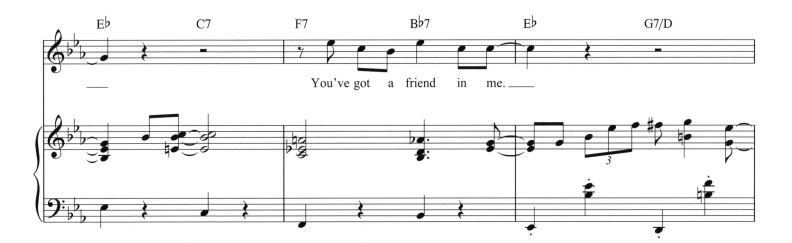

ZIP-A-DEE-DOO-DAH

from SONG OF THE SOUTH

Words by RAY GILBERT
Music by ALLIE WRUBEL

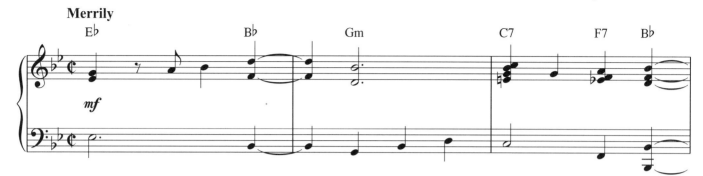

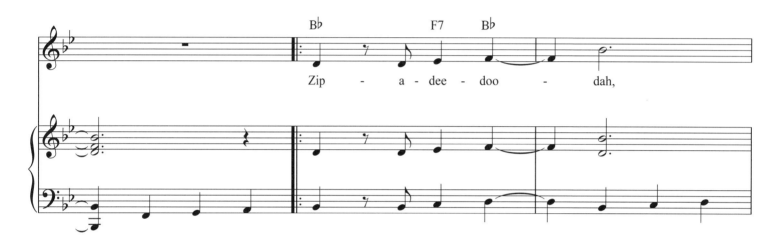

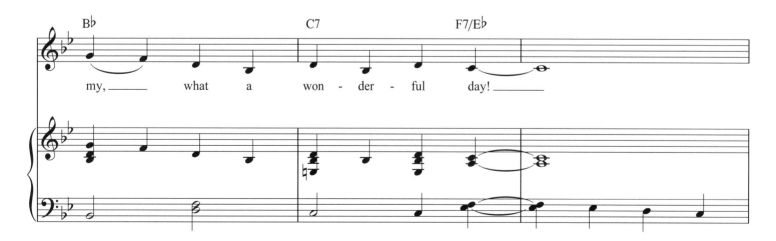

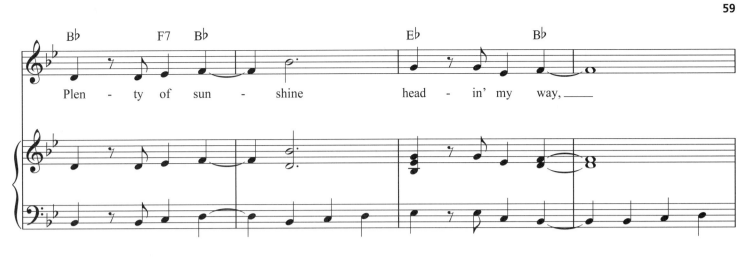

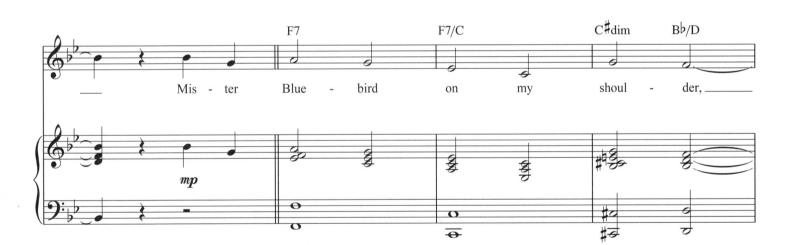

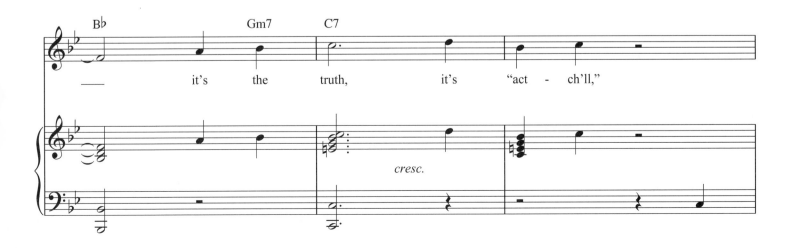

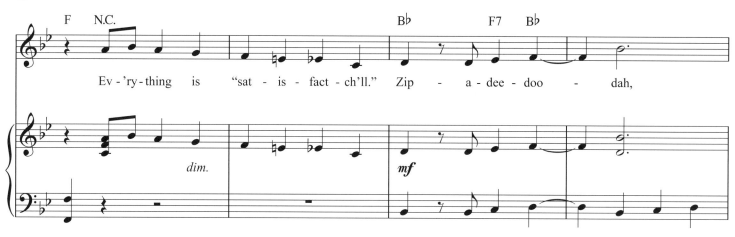

Ev-'ry-thing is "sat-is-fact-ch'll." Zip - a-dee-doo - dah,

zip - a-dee - ay! _____ Won - der-ful feel -

- ing, won - der-ful day. _____

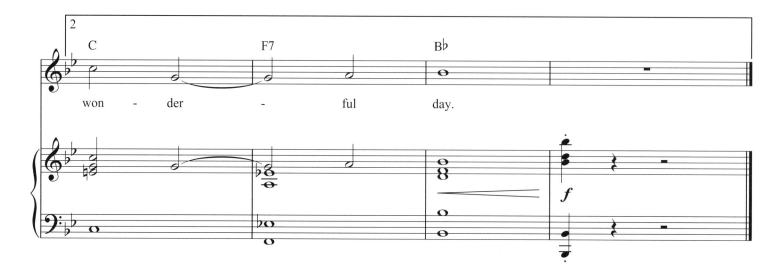

won - der - ful day.

Whether you're a karaoke singer or an auditioning professional, the **Pro Vocal®** series is for you! Unlike most karaoke packs, each book in the Pro Vocal series contains the lyrics, melody, and chord symbols for at least eight hit songs. The audio contains demos for listening, and separate backing tracks so you can sing along. Perfect for home rehearsal, parties, auditions, corporate events, and gigs without a backup band.

WOMEN'S EDITIONS

MEN'S EDITIONS

EXERCISES

MIXED EDITIONS

These editions feature songs for both male and female voices.

KIDS EDITIONS

Visit Hal Leonard online at
www.halleonard.com

HAL•LEONARD®

Prices, contents, & availability subject to change without notice.

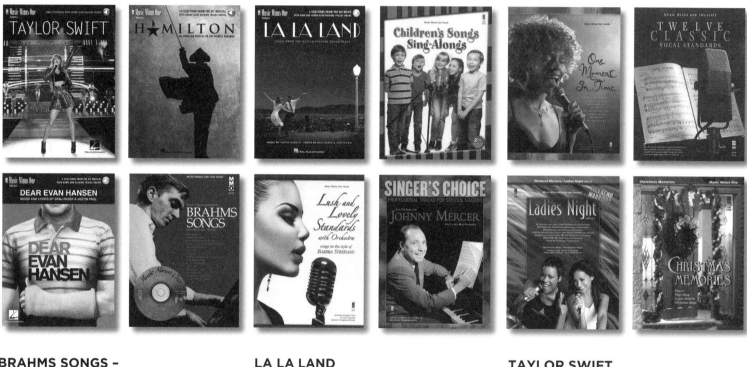